FRASER VALLEY

JOSEF HANUS & JOSEF M. HANUS

Personal gift to:

From:

CW00393501

Lillooet Valley

The Fraser River, entering the valley by Lillooet, springs some 1200 kilometres away in the Rocky Mountains. This book covers the trip from Lillooet and Hope, through Chilliwack, Abbotsford, Surrey, Langley, White Rock, Richmond and Delta on the left bank, and on the right bank, Harrison, Maple Ridge, Pitt Meadows, Coquitlam, Port Coquitlam, New Westminster and Queensborough.

Lillooet

Lillooet, a town of 2900, is the first stop in this book's journey through the Fraser Valley. We visited the Miyaziki Heritage House, the Lillooet Museum, the Hangman's Tree and Chinese Rock Pilings.

Cariboo Highway

The Cariboo Highway (Hwy 12) connects Lytton and Lillooet through breathtaking countryside, with the Stein Valley to the west and Epsom Provincial Park to the east. This area is Gold Rush country. Lillooet is Mile '0' of the Gold Rush Trail. Our trip through the Fraser River Valley started here in the Lillooet area, as featured on the first two pages of this book.

St. Andrew's – St. Mary's

Lillooet, situated on the banks of the Fraser River, was founded as Mile '0' of the famous Cariboo Trail. Gold seekers used this route to reach the interior. This picture is of St. Andrew's – St. Mary's Church, located in the town centre.

Kanaka

The Cantilever Range and the Fraser Canyon are the subject of this picture, taken by Kanaka Bar. The Kanakas were Hawaiian Islanders brought by a Hudson Bay Company trading ship to British Columbia around 1840.

Kanaka Bar

Kanaka Bar is a popular stop for truckers travelling the old and scenic Trans-Canada Highway 1. The native Thompson name for Kanaka Bar means "crossing place."

Fountain Ridge

The valley and river near Riley Creek was photographed close to Lillooet. The area between Lillooet and Hope is known for its hot and dry climate and for its deer hunting. Both the Fraser River and Thompson River by Lytton are famous for river rafting.

Seton Lake

Brilliantly coloured Seton Lake, best known for its trout fishing, is located by Lillooet in the southern part of Cariboo Country. The green waters of Seton Lake empty into the Fraser River via a spawning channel by the town of Lillooet.

Anderson River

Two railways follow the Fraser River, the Canadian Pacific and the Canadian National. This picture of the railway bridge was taken by Anderson River, located near Boston Bar. The campground is located by the confluence of the Anderson and Fraser Rivers.

Boston Bar

Originally a popular stop during the gold rush midway between Lytton and Yale, here a busy roadhouse was joined by several homes, a store, a hotel and a restaurant. The place still remains a popular stop for travellers. Like other towns on the Fraser River, Boston Bar began because gold was discovered in the area.

Lytton

The place where the clear green waters of the Thompson River meet with the brown, silt-laden Fraser River, Lytton is famed as the Rafting Capital of Canada. Other 'tamer' activities such as hiking, camping and fishing can be enjoyed in close proximity to the town.

Thompson River

This autumn picture of the Thompson River was taken in Skihist Provincial Park near Lytton, where the Thompson River empties into the Fraser River. The Thompson River springs from the North Thompson Oxbows Manteau Provincial Park in the Columbia Mountains, close to the British Columbia–Alberta boundary.

Alexandra Bridge

Three bridges have spanned the river twenty kilometres north of Yale, close to Spuzzum. The first one was named for the Princess of Wales, Alexandra. The second one still exists on the site. The newest bridge is shown in the larger picture.

Old Bridge

Physical evidence of the scale of transport through the Fraser Canyon before 1950 can be seen in the old Alexandra Bridge. Constructed in 1863, the bridge served until 1964, when it was closed to vehicles and the new bridge was opened for traffic.

Hell's Gate

An impressive fall view of the Fraser Canyon at the place where the canyon is at its narrowest—some 30 metres wide. The gorge here is 180 metres deep and the river moves at 7 metres per second. Hell's Gate is a popular tourist stop and the opposite bank of the river can be reached using the Hell's Gate Airtram. A bypass around turbulent waters for spawning salmon was constructed via fish ladders in 1945. A unique view of spawning fish can be observed from the suspension bridge.

Emory Creek Park

On this page, the area around the Fraser River by Yale is considered to be the starting point of the Gold Rush Trail.

Fraser Canyon

The longest British Columbian river springs from Mount Robson Provincial Park, under Simon Peak. Its journey through British Columbia covers over 1350 km, until the river empties into the Pacific Ocean by Richmond.

Hell's Gate Tunnel

Seven tunnels were built on Highway 1 between Yale and Hell's Gate. Pictured here is Hell's Tunnel, located by Black Canyon.

Yale

One of the oldest communities in British Columbia is nestled where the mighty Fraser Canyon begins. Yale had 30,000 citizens during the height of the Gold Rush. Today, just 200 people live in the district. In this picture is the church of St. John the Divine, the oldest house of worship on its original site in British Columbia's mainland. The church was built by miners in 1860. The Fraser River is intimately connected with the Gold Rush. The river served to transport the prospectors to the gold fields. Yale, whose banks are the subject of the smaller picture on page 9, became the largest town west of Chicago and north of San Francisco in the gold rush of 1856. Also pictured are the Cascade Mountains, looming silently above the rows of Yale Cemetery.

Hope Mountain

Here are the Fraser River, Hope and Hope Mountain above the town. This small community, hidden in the forest under the mountains, is our first stop after a two-hundred–kilometre journey from Merritt and Kamloops. Here, the Trans-Canada Highway 1 splits into three highways. The Yellowhead (No. 3) runs through Manning Park to Princeton, the Coquihalla Highway (No. 5) runs to Merritt, Kelowna and Kamloops, and No. 1 leads travellers to Lytton, Lillooet, Cache Creek and Kamloops.

Hope

The Japanese Friendship Garden and Hope's town centre are the subject of the two smaller photographs.

Gold Rush Trail

The forested mountains surrounding Hope and Yale are filled with spectacular trails for hikers of all ages. This photograph was taken in Kawkawa Lake Provincial Park, close to Jorgenson Peak. The Hope Visitor Information Centre has good trail maps and guides available for visitors.

Hope

Hope, the gateway between Greater Vancouver and the rest of British Columbia is also known as the Chainsaw Carving Capital of the World. This small and friendly community of 7000 residents is nestled under the Coast Mountains. The statue of the Gold Seeker is found in the city centre.

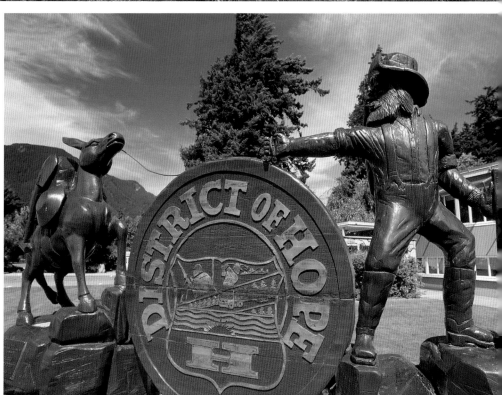

Coquihalla Canyon

The Coquihalla Canyon Provincial Park and the abandoned Othello Quintette Tunnels of the railway are well known Hope attractions. Coquihalla Canyon, pictured in the larger photograph, is a part of the Cascade Mountains. The tunnels are a part of the Kettle Valley Railway and were designed by engineer Andrew McCulloch.

Hope

Hope's unique carvings charm both locals and visitors alike. Two dozen beautiful carvings were created by Hope's chainsaw carver Pete Ryan, from trees which were removed from Memorial Park because of root rot.

Aerial View

This aerial view of the eastern part of the Fraser Valley was taken from an altitude of 5000 metres. Harrison Lake and Hemlock Mountains are clearly visible in this picture.

Silverhope Creek

Twinkling in the mountains by Chilliwack Lake, Silverhope Creek is well stocked with rainbow and brook trout.

Hope Slide

Johnson Peak is an infamous point on Manson Ridge, just 15 kilometres from Hope. On January 9, 1965, its stones became a grave for four people in their three cars who were passing through the area at the worst possible time. A massive landslide of 60 million cubic yards—a 60–metre depth of stone, trees and mud—swept the valley of Nicolum Creek, and across the highway. The extent of the damage is still clearly visible.

Trails

The hiking trails around Hope are a hiker's paradise. Hundreds of locals and Vancouverites often come to visit their favourite spots.

Silver Lake

Located close to Hope and hidden under Mount Stoneman and Wells Peak, Silver Lake is some 12 km from the highway. A dusty gravel road will bring you to this beautiful place with cool water and lovely beaches. A popular camping destination.

Flood

This autumn picture was taken by the small community of Flood, nestled by the Fraser River between Laidlaw and Silver Creek.

Fraser River

The Fraser River, seen here by the Agassiz–Rosedale Bridge, springs from Mount Robson Provincial Park. After a long journey passing Prince George, Williams Lake and Lillooet, the river roars into the Fraser Valley. The river was the first route into the province, bringing early fur traders and gold prospectors. The river was named after explorer Simon Fraser, who travelled it in 1808 with several North West Company men from Prince George.

Seabird Island

Salmon fishing on the Fraser River is world famous. The salmon season starts every year in May with the chinook salmon run.

Fisherman's Paradise

When the river is open for sockeye in late July or early August, thousands of fishermen occupy the river's best spots on its beaches and islands. Millions of sockeye and king salmon spawn in the Fraser River and its tributaries, bringing good fishing for all sports and commercial fishermen. Those fish which are not caught continue at a speed of 30 km daily farther up the river to the tributaries and lakes where they were hatched four years previously.

Scale Bar

Stony beaches around Croft Island are full of fishermen and their families, enjoying beautiful sunny days and good fishing.

Chehalis River

The crisp clear waters of the Chehalis River flow from Chehalis Lake. The river is well known among local fishermen and is heavily visited in the fall and winter months for salmon and later for steelhead fishing. The river connects Chehalis Lake with the Harrison and Fraser Rivers.

Lake Errock

This winter picture of a frozen creek was taken near Lake Errock, close to Kilby Provincial Park.

Chilliwack Countryside

Cheam Peak majestically stands over the Fraser Valley. The countryside near Gill Beach is the subject of this picture.

Kent

District of Kent is a county with 5000 citizens. Bordered by the Fraser River, Kent is comprised of the communities Chehalis, Agassiz, Harrison Mills, Seabird Island and Kent. The arrival of the railway in 1881 encouraged settlers who began farming and fishing. Agriculture and tourism are still the main economic activity of Kent citizens. Kent is heavily visited during summer months, Harrison Lake being one of the most popular vacation spots in British Columbia.

Four Brothers

This scenic picture of Four Brothers Mountain bordering the plains of the Fraser Valley was taken by Cheam View.

Laidlaw

The meadows in bloom on the banks of the Fraser River are beautiful in spring. This shot of the bank of the Fraser River was taken close to Laidlaw. A local attraction is the Doll Museum. Laidlaw is located by Mount Devoy, just 17 km west of Hope.

Bridal Falls

Chilliwack's most striking view is the 122–metre high Bridal Veil Falls. A ten minute hike from the parking lot will lead visitors to the base of the impressive cascade. At the lowest part, the waterfall is a 25–metre high curtain of water. The picnic area and hiking trails in the forest around the falls offer the more adventurous a recreational family activity for the whole day. Bridal Falls is 17 kilometres from Chilliwack, and the entrance is from the junction of Highways #1 and #9.

Mount Archibald

Bridal Falls Provincial Park is located in the mountains of the Skagit Range, just under Mount Archibald (1729 m).

23

Queens Island

A rainbow above the Fraser River, Chilliwack, Sardis and Queens Island is visible in this picture, taken from the Kilby Provincial Park, just above Deroche. The mountains in the back are the Skagit Range.

Fairfield Island

The meadows and fields near Chilliwack are green even in December. This scene shows a ranch on Fairfield Island. Visible is Cheam Peak with Knight Peak and Conway Peak on the left side.

Minter Garden

32–acre Minter Garden is well known floral artistry by the Agassiz–Rosedale Highway. Nestled against white Mt. Cheam, the Garden was begun by the Minter family in 1980. After the gorgeous yellow slopes of daffodils fade, over 100,000 tulips imported from Holland grace the garden, well organised into 11 theme gardens, and in a myriad of colours. A thousand rhododendrons are planted in the garden, and specifically in the Rhododendron Garden. Located 90 minutes from Vancouver, the garden is a favourite spot for weddings. A long list of events such as the Mother's Day Celebration, the Rose Extravaganza and Autumn Colours are organized.

Hunter Creek

A walking trail by Hunter Creek.

Slesse River

Slesse River flows from the North Cascades National Park and empties as a tributary into the Chilliwack River. The woods of Slesse Mountain and the pebbled bed of the river create a peaceful scene.

Saint Thomas

The lovely architecture of the Saint Thomas Episcopalian Church, located in Chilliwack by Young Road and First Avenue..

Fraser Valley

This greenbelt of berry fields, meadows, farmlands, pleasant towns and pastures east of Vancouver is a central part of the Fraser Valley. Chilliwack, Sardis, and smaller surrounding communities, all nestled along the Fraser River, were photographed from Lookout Ridge by Sardis. Nicomen Mountain and Deroche Mountain are visible on the horizon.

Hog Island

A countryside view from Hog Island, close to Chilliwack. In the background are the Nicomen Mountains, located on the opposite side of the Fraser River.

Skagit Range

Chilliwack Lake and the mountains of the Skagit Range, Mount Webb, McDonald Peak and Mount Lindeman are seen in this photograph, taken from Chilliwack Lake Provincial Park.

Yarrow

This spring picture of an orchard was photographed in a private garden, close to Yarrow.

Vedder River

The Vedder–Chilliwack River flows out from Chilliwack Lake some 50 km north of Sardis. The river runs along the beautiful, changing scenery of the Skagit Range. Numerous campsites entice tourists to stay in the forest by the river bank. Hikers, kayakers and anglers enjoy the river year round. Above Tamahi Bridge is a kayakers' competition course. Salmon and steelhead fishing here is fantastic. The river has 36 km of fishable water. The Vedder–Chilliwack River is the most popular recreational river in the Lower Mainland.

Chilliwack Museum

Built in 1912, the exquisite building of the former City Hall is now a heritage site, and hosts the Chilliwack Museum. In addition to regular exhibits, the museum houses some 10,000 photographs, maps, sound recordings and books.

Chilliwack Lake

Next to Cultus Lake, Chilliwack Lake is the most visited recreational area in the Fraser Valley by water lovers in summer and hikers in winter. The lake's campsites are fully occupied from May to October and some campers enjoy the lake in winter months. Chilliwack River is famous for its salmon and steelhead fishing from August to March. The lake, Paleface Mountain and Mount Meroniuk are seen in the first picture.

St. Theresa

St. Theresa Church is located on Chilliwack River Road.

Rosedale

The Rosedale United Church is located on Yale Road East.

Cheam Peak

A bridge on the Agassiz–Rosedale Highway, the Fraser River, Ferry Island, Cheam Peak and Lady Peak are pictured in this early spring photograph taken from the north Fraser River bank from Whorlley Lane in Agassiz.

Sardis

Cottonwood Mall in Sardis.

Promontory

Promontory is a part of Chilliwack located in the hills by Lookout Ridge and Chilliwack River Provincial Park. Promontory gives a great view over the Chilliwack Valley.

Cultus Lake

The natural paradise of Cultus Lake Park lures thousands of visitors yearly. Located just a few minutes from Chilliwack, the lake's 600 acres are open to all water lovers. Besides kilometres of beaches, there are four campgrounds with hundreds of campsites, several picnic areas, and golf courses located by the beaches.

Lindell Beach

A small community on the southern shore of Cultus Lake, Lindell Beach is an extremely beautiful place to live. The gardens of these homes are located just by the lake shore and residents have the beach right by their doors.

Columbia Valley

Travelling south, colourful meadows and a friendly countryside of ranches just a few kilometres of Cultus Lake will surround you. Columbia Valley is flanked by International Ridge Provincial Park on the left and by Vedder Mountain on the right.

Beaches

The beaches of Cultus and Chilliwack Lakes are a favourite destination of locals, Fraser Valley residents and vacationers in hot summer months. Numerous campsites and campgrounds in this area are fully occupied from May to October. These sunbathers, residents from Chilliwack, were photographed by Cultus Lake.

Chilliwack River

Chilliwack River is a salmon fishing paradise, the most popular river in Fraser Valley. The river runs through a lovely valley past the Skagit Range. The fishable part of the river is 36 km long and starts under Slesse Creek. This picture was taken by the Tamahi Bridge, another favourite spot of fishermen. The spring salmon season starts in July, coho enters the river in September, together with spring, chum and others. Fall and winter steelhead fishing is famous—the river is the most productive steelhead river in the Lower Mainland.

Chilliwack Downtown

A new clock tower complements the courthouse located at Five Corners. Chilliwack is the city of festivals, with marketplaces, parades and historical celebrations. The third picture, taken on Spadina Avenue, shows the Chilliwack United Church, which has served the community since 1865.

Chilliwack

Nestled in the upper Fraser Valley, Chilliwack is an important industrial and agricultural part of the Lower Mainland. A major attraction is the Chilliwack Fall Exhibition, held in mid-August. A diorama of the Battle of Waterloo is displayed in The Royal Canadian Engineers Military Museum. The Landing Leisure Centre with its aquatic centre and aerobic studio, fitness and wellness centre is a common family destination. This picture of Chilliwack was taken from the hill above the city.

Chilliwack

The First Christian Reformed Church and the city street with the court are photographed in the two smaller pictures.

Sardis

The busy and friendly community of Sardis is located on the southern side of the Trans-Canada Highway. This view was taken from Promontory Road. Some local parks are Wells Landing Park, Sardis Sports Field and Kinkora Golf Course.

University College

Home to more than 6500 students, the University College of the Fraser Valley in Chilliwack has three flagship programs: health sciences, agriculture and theatre. The university has three campuses, in Chilliwack, Abbotsford and Mission. Shakespeare Garden, in the picture, was created by university students.

Golf Courses

Chilliwack is a superb destination for serious and amateur golfers. Thanks to its mild climate, Chilliwack has over 10 evergreen golf courses, mostly open year round. The Royalwood Golf Course, located by Vedder canal and Trans-Canada Highway, is shown in the larger picture.

Arnold Countryside

The Fraser Valley reveals some beautiful vistas to travellers. Barns, new and old, are seen everywhere with farm houses and cottages. The Fraser Valley is the main food provider for almost two million people living in Greater Vancouver and the Lower Mainland.

Mill Lake

This small lake and two parks in the centre of Abbotsford are the most relaxing places in the city. Centennial Park and John Mahoney Park are located around the lake just metres from the Seven Oaks Shopping Centre and South Fraser Way. Close to Mill Lake is the MSA Heritage Museum, a running track, and public elementary and secondary schools.

New Abbotsford

Abbotsford is the fifth largest British Columbian municipality. Laid out in 1889, the city takes its name from Harry Abbott, the general superintendent of the Canadian Pacific Railway. In 2003, Abbotsford's population reached 120,000 people. Both pictures were taken in the centre of Abbotsford, a park by City Hall and Clearbrook Library, and Gladwin Road.

Mount Baker

The most visible landmark in the Fraser Valley, Mount Baker is actually located in the Washington State. The Fraser Valley was first settled around Abbotsford and Sumas and the area is known as the heart of Fraser Valley. This photograph was taken from Sumas Way and shows Sumas Mountain, the newly-developed Abbotsford neighbour, Yale, and a beautifully lit Mount Baker in the background.

Abbotsford–Yale

A new development in Abbotsford by Sumas Way and Marshall Road by Yale is pictured on the second photograph. The area is located on Sumas Mountain on the eastern side of the city.

Matsqui Trail

The Mission Bridge Picnic Area and the Matsqui Trail, both just metres from Matsqui Village, are favoured by salmon fishermen and hikers. The bridge is a boundary between salt water and fresh water. The Matsqui Trail, which begins in Olund Park, runs by the river to Page Road and is 13 km long. This picture was taken by the CP Rail Bridge and Mission Bridge.

Abbotsford – Sumas Mt.

In the second and third pictures, new houses in Abbotsford on Sumas Mountain, showing Delair Road and Kilgard with the Pacific Coast Mountain Range in the background.

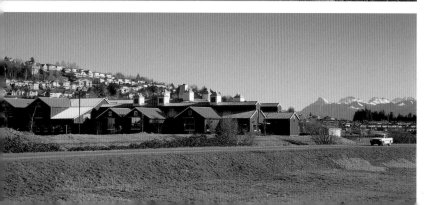

40

Abbotsford Airshow

Since 1962, the Abbotsford Airshow is held every year for three days in the beginning of August at the Abbotsford Airport. The first airshow attracted 15,000 spectators. Now, the International Airshow—recognised as the biggest and finest in the world—attracts almost half a million spectators. Almost 1000 aircraft ranging from vintage biplanes to modern jets perform the finest aero-acrobatics, and professionals perform breathtaking exhibitions. In the picture are the Canadian Forces Snowbirds. The Airport is situated in the western part of Matsqui Municipality.

Exhibition Park

This picture shows the Abbotsford Agrifair.

Abbotsford Agrifair

The largest summer agricultural fair in British Columbia, the Agrifair is held in the first days of August in Abbotsford–Clearbrook in the CFV Exhibition Park. Abbotsford's first fair was held in Gifford, in 1911. The Fair has been held at its present location since 1981. Family oriented events include pro rodeo, pig races, livestock competitions and various displays. Younger visitors also come for the Midway Carnival.

Fraser Rodeo

The Mighty Fraser Bud Pro Rodeo is the popular Abbotsford Agrifair event. The rodeo was added to the fair's show in 1988. The finest cowboys compete in bull riding, saddle bronco riding, steer wrestling, bareback riding and calf roping.

Clayburn Village

Clayburn was founded by Charles Maclure in 1905. The village is located 5 kilometres northeast of Abbotsford. Shown here, the Pioneer Clayburn Church served the community from 1912 to 1958. Clayburn Heritage Days provide entertainment, contests and the opening of heritage homes, art exhibits and old-fashioned children's games. The Clayburn Store, photographed in the smaller picture, is a fine example of resourceful use of a heritage building. Visitors can enjoy sandwiches, a cheese dish or tea, while children enjoy the old fashioned English candy. Clayburn Village remains a residential community.

Abbotsford–Clearbrook

The library in Abbotsford's Clearbrook district is a favourite destination of locals and students. The library is located by South Fraser Way and Trethewey Street, neighbouring Municipality House and the Abbotsford Police Department building in the park.

South Fraser Way

Transportation, agriculture and precision manufacturing are the main industries of Abbotsford residents—95% of them work in the city or in surrounding communities. South Fraser Way is Abbotsford's main street and the city's centre. All important businesses and shopping are located along it. The third picture shows the Seven Oaks Mall with Mount Baker in the background. Downtown can be quickly reached from the Trans-Canada Highway and the exit from South Fraser Way to the highway is easily accessible.

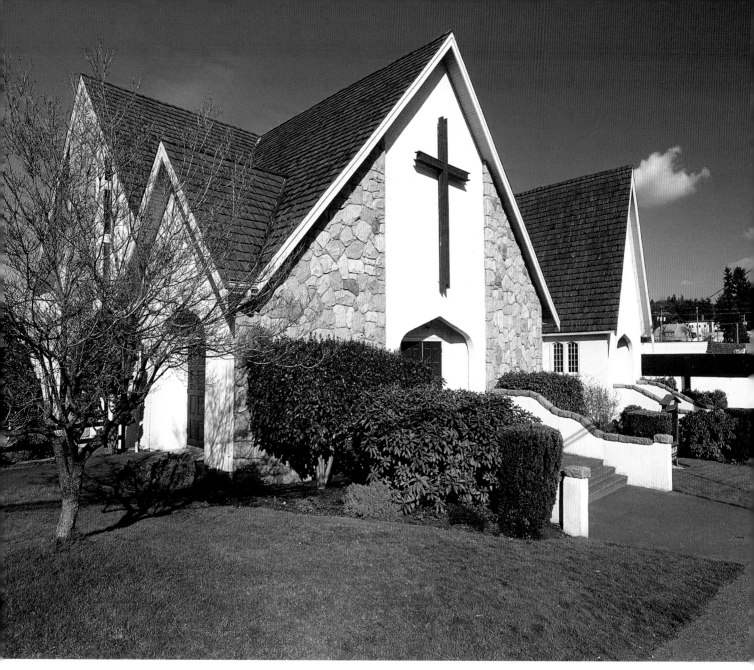

Abbotsford

The first settlement in the area was in Sumas Valley. The city was one of the fastest growing areas in North America. Around 1867, the farms produced milk and tobacco. One interesting point is that the Fraser Valley has in its centre a 1,500 metre thick layer of rich soil, which the river carried into the British Columbian interior plateau over 50 million years. Pictured here is Abbotsford's Trinity Memorial United Church located on Hazel Street.

Huntington

The Huntington countryside.

Matsqui Prairie

Farms are everywhere in the Matsqui Prairie between the Fraser River and Abbotsford. Dairy farms and milk-processing plants are a major part of the Fraser Valley industry. It is hard to believe that the Fraser River needed 'just' 50 million years to create this land of rich soil.

Abbotsford – Clayburn

The view from Sumas Mountain shows a part of Abbotsford and Matsqui Prairie with Clayburn Village on the right side. From Abbotsford farms come 80% of British Columbian eggs and 90% of Canada's raspberries.

Sumas Mountain

Sumas Mountain on the horizon and the Fraser River by Mission are shown in this picture, taken from the Mission waterfront close to the bridge connecting Mission with Matsqui District and Abbotsford. The Sumas Mountain Provincial Park in the background is the eastern border of the Fraser Valley.

Mission

Mission is located by the Fraser River, on the opposite side from Matsqui Prairie. In 1861, a French priest, Father Fouquet, founded the St. Mary's Indian Residential School on the site, where downtown Mission is now. Thirty years later, the area was incorporated as the Municipality of Mission. North Railway Avenue is in this picture.

Fraser by Mission

Abbotsford and Mission's main and only connector is the Abbotsford–Mission Bridge spanning the Fraser River, pictured on this page.

Mission

Home to 32,000 residents, Mission is located on the north shore of the Fraser River, just 70 kilometres east of Vancouver. Various attractions include the Mission Raceway, the Mission Folk Music Festival, the Clarke Foundation Theatre and the Heritage Park Centre. These pictures show the old city's First Avenue and Railway Avenue.

Fraser by Kent

Bringing both rich soil and pioneers to the area, the Fraser River was an important link during the Cariboo Gold Rush. The Fraser is 1368 km long, stretching from its source in Mt. Robson Park to its emptying into the Pacific Ocean by Richmond. This picture was taken by Chilliwack and shows the river and Kent on the opposite riverbank. The District of Kent is larger than the City of Vancouver, but it is mainly an agricultural area with hazelnut orchards, dairy farms and hundreds of acres of corn. Agassiz is the administrative and shopping centre for the district.

Hemlock Mountain

The winter playground of the Fraser Valley is Hemlock Valley, hidden high in a natural bowl on Hemlock Mountain. Local skiers can avoid hours of travel to distant winter recreational centres, as the area is easily reached from Harrison Mills. Ideal snow condition exist here during the whole winter, as the day lodge is situated at 975 metres and the area receives up to 200 cm of snow annually. Seven kilometres of pristine trails bring enjoyment to adults and children. Hemlock Valley is open on Fridays and weekends.

Norris Creek

Hidden under Nicomen Mountain at the end of Old Hawkinson Way in Deroche and running between hills and mountains, the creek flows deep and clear with ideal conditions for salmon fishing on one side of the bridge, and with kilometres of stony flats on the other. This is a paradise for hikers and fly-fishers, while numerous black bears can be observed from spring until the winter months.

Cascade Peninsula

Cascade Mountain, located on a peninsula in Harrison Lake and Cascade Bay, is photographed from the Sasquatch Provincial Park.

Weaver Lake

The Cascade Mountains and Weaver Lake were photographed from Mount Keenan. The way to Hemlock Valley Ski Resort offers a lovely view of the area around Harrison Lake, which is hidden in the valley just behind Weaver Lake.

Rainbow Falls

The best way to enjoy the beauty of Harrison Lake is by walking. A gravel road around Harrison Lake offers a fine view of the lake and its wild surroundings. Harrison Beach Lagoon is reached by parking by the lakefront. Over 12 trails built on old logging roads offer fine recreational opportunities (see page 88).

Harrison Lake

Harrison Lake offers countless views and beautiful beaches. This spring picture of Harrison Lake, Long Island and Mount McRae was taken from Cogburn Beach near Bear Creek. Clean stone beaches offer rest and a view of the clear lake waters.

Kilby

Located at Harrison Mills in Kent county, the Kilby General Store Museum awaits visitors with its unique local architecture and a taste of the 1900's. Thomas Kilby opened his store and hotel in 1904, where visitors can now spend money for memorabilia and gifts.

Blueberry Farm

Blueberries are the most common fruit grown in the Fraser Valley. This blueberry field was photographed by Dewdney, and Nicomen Mountain is in the background.

Hope Countryside

Countryside by Sasquatch Provincial Park and Sacred Heart Church, located on Chawathill Road.

Cascade Bay

65 km–long Harrison Lake is bigger than it appears from Harrison Hot Springs, and it connects with Lillooet Lake via the Lillooet River. It was a well used Native trade route around 1850 and later played a part in the Cariboo gold rush with sternwheeler traffic. A gravel road running around Harrison Lake is not in very good condition, but a four wheel drive vehicle should not be necessary. The view of the lake and beaches, reached after 20 km, will reward you with pure unspoiled beauty. This picture was taken from the forestry campground, located by Slollicum Creek on Cascade Bay.

Harrison Hot Springs

Mineral hot springs, rich with sulphur and potash are a major draw for this small Fraser Valley town. Water cooled to 37°C is piped into two indoor and one outdoor pool. The sand on the town's beaches was dredged from the lakebed.

Dewdney Peak

Dewdney Peak is 920 metres high, rising above Dewdney. Dewdney Trunk Road starts in Maple Ridge by 201 Street and runs to Hatzic. The small community of Dewdney is located where the Lougheed Highway crosses Nicomen Slough.

Nicomen Mountain

Nicomen Slough and Nicomen Mountain (1225 m), are shown in the second picture.

Deroche

Fall brings both gorgeous colours and beautiful morning fog. Photography, fishing and hunting are pleasant activities, it being enough just to be outside. This picture was taken on the slopes of Deroche Mountain.

Agassiz

Gold prospector Captain L. N. Agassiz settled in the area in 1867. From him the area takes its name. Corn and dairy are the main industries of this small community. In these pictures is an Agassiz Museum and the Pacific Agriculture Research Centre. Some 1800-metre–high peaks above the Fraser Valley are covered with snow and glaciers. Millions of years ago, the underlying area was ocean. Dutch immigrants started by draining the flood plains and landscaped the fields. Today this area is known as the "Corn Capital of BC." The community is located close to Harrison Hot Springs.

Golden Ears Park

A hiking picture from the side of Mount Blanshard in Golden Ears Provincial Park. The 55,000—hectare park has snow-covered peaks 1700 metres high. Interesting hiking trails lead into a forest of Douglas Fir, Hemlock, Balsam and Western Red Cedar. Another picture of Golden Ears Mountain is on page 66—Katzie Slough.

Raven Lake

Located in Golden Ears Provincial Park, small and beautiful Raven Lake is difficult to reach.

Rolley Lake

A small popular lake close to Mission, located in Rolley Lake Provincial Park. Summer visitors enjoy camping in the surrounding forest and picnicking on the beach.

Sasquatch Park

An autumn picture taken in Sasquatch Country, located on the mountain slopes by Harrison Lake. The legendary monster named "Sasquatch" lives in the park, but is seldom seen by tourists and hikers. More likely sights are great blue herons, bald eagles, deer or black bears.

Westminster Abbey

A Benedictine monastery with its impressive 51 metre–tall Pfitzer bell tower is located above Mission, on Mount Mary Ann. The whole area of Mission, Hatzic, Fraser River and Matsqui Prairie can be seen from a viewpoint by the monastery.

Stave River

Salmon fishing on Stave River a short outlet from Hayward Lake. There are no lifeguards on duty at Hayward, Stave, and Ruskin recreation areas and changes in river levels can occur without warning.

Stave Lake

Camping, fishing for cat trout, hiking, and more is offered to those who spend some time in the area around Stave Lake. A good gravel road which starts by Stave Falls carries forestry workers via heavy transport on weekdays, and runs some 20 km around the lake. The last part is suitable only for 4-wheel drive, and leads travellers around three small lakes—Devils Lake, Sayers Lake and Florence Lake—and finally finishes by the northern end of Alouette Lake

Xá:ytem

9000 years of history and culture is represented by thousands of artifacts in one of British Columbia's oldest known dwelling sites. An enormous rock, one of the Fraser Valley's most famous transformer stones, is the focal point of Xá:ytem. Sto:lo oral history explains that the rock was once three men who had defied the wishes of the Creator.

61

Davis Lake Park

Stave Lake with Davis Lake Provincial Park and Mount Benedict in the background are the subjects of this picture, taken from Mount Crickmer. Davis Lake Park is a part of Douglas Forest. Stave Lake is located by Golden Ears Provincial Park, close to Mission.

Hatzic Lake

Summer cottages are spread along the peninsula in Hatzic Lake, located between Dewdney and Mission.

Hatzic

The small community of Hatzic, photographed with the Fraser River from Westminster Abbey close to Mission.

Hayward Lake

This fall picture of the lowest part of Stave Lake shows Hayward Lake. Hayward Lake and Ruskin are well-known and heavily-visited fishing destinations in the area. Hayward Lake Reservoir offers the 10-kilometre Reservoir Trail, and the 6-kilometre Railway Trail; both are open for hiking and biking.

Albion

The eastern part of Maple Ridge, Albion is located on the bank of the Fraser River by McMillan Island.

Fort Langley

Fort Langley is a town rich with history, offering a glimpse into the oldest permanent European settlement in the Pacific Northwest. "Derby" was the first name used for this site, intending it to become the capital of British Columbia. Governor Sir James Douglas proclaimed the 'Colony of British Columbia' in 1858, and Fort Langley become the birth place of British Columbia. An historic document, a photograph of this ceremony exists in Fort Langley.

Maple Ridge

Located by the Fraser River by the Mountain Forest and under Alouette Mountain, Maple Ridge and Haney are the centre of this lovely part of the Fraser Valley. An aerial picture was taken from some 400 metres above and shows the city centre, Port Haney Wharf, the Fraser River and Derby Reach Regional Park on the opposite side, close to Fort Langley. Good places to visit are the Fraser River Heritage Walk, the Maple Ridge Museum, historic Haney and some historic buildings of Port Haney's, such as St. Andrew's Heritage Church, the old 1911 Bank of Montreal, the Japanese kindergarten from 1930 or the Masonic Hall. The name Maple Ridge comes from the ridge of maple trees, a grove on Maclivor's dairy farm.

Parsons Channel

Barnston Island Ferry on Parsons Channel in the second picture.

Albion Ferry

The Albion Ferry (third picture) connects Fort Langley and Maple Ridge for cars and pedestrians at no charge.

Alouette River

The Alouette River springs forth from Golden Ears Provincial Park. A pleasant walk along the river will lead you to the southern bank of Alouette Lake. It is within easy reach and an easy walk for a family trip.

Katzie Slough

Katzie Slough and Golden Ears Provincial Park are shown on this page. The area is known for its long and easy walks.

Pitt Meadows

Pitt Meadows is a fertile agricultural lowland between the slopes of Port Coquitlam and the forested hills of Maple Ridge. Berry fields and dairy farms cover its vast fields. The dikes along the Pitt River offer easy flat walks. Canoeists enjoy the rivers in Pitt Meadows, Pitt River, Katzie Slough and Alouette River. With nearby Maple Ridge, the area is known as the Horse Capital of Canada. Wooded pastures in Maple Ridge are crossed by 170 kilometres of riding trails.

Haney–Pitt Meadows

An aerial shot showing the Lougheed Highway and 203 Street, where Pitt Meadows and Maple Ridge meet.

McMillan Island

Fort Langley and McMillan Island, pictured from above.

Fort Langley

The fur trading post of Fort Langley, part of the Hudson's Bay Company's network, was established in 1827. The growth of the fort continued up to 1839, when it was completed in 1841. The original fort was abandoned 45 years later. When New Westminster was established as the capital, the commercial importance of Fort Langley was eclipsed and in 1886 Fort Langley closed. This small town offers visitors a taste of the 1850's. Points of interest in the town are the Station, City Hall, St. George Church and the Fort itself. Lovely cafés and a bountiful antique market line its pretty streets. In 1858, miners struck gold in the Fraser Valley. Within a month, 20,000 gold seekers flooded through the Hudson's Bay Company's Fort Langley, threatening the peace in this formerly sleepy trading post.

Pitt Lake

Located by Golden Ears Provincial Park, Pitt Lake is a common destination for boaters and sport fishermen.

St. George

The picturesque pastoral town of Fort Langley, the first capital of British Columbia, is located east of Vancouver on the south shore of the Fraser River. Today it is the Fort Langley National Historic Site, evoking the spirit of the frontier. Summer programs offer history lessons with demonstrations, films and activities. The celebration of Fort Langley's Past is popular, as is Heritage Week, held at the end of February. Crafts, games, guided strolls, a slide show and exhibits are offered to visitors. On the smaller picture is the St. George Church, located two blocks from Glower Road. On the opposite page are photographs of the town's City Hall and Store House in the heritage site.

Haney Place

European settlers arrived in 1858 and began the task of transforming rainforest into farmland. The first two pioneers were John Maclivor and Samuel Robertson from Scotland. In 1874, more men and families came to purchase land, which was priced at $1 per acre. This price had the condition that the settler set up residency and clear the land for farming within three years. Haney is a part of the District of Maple Ridge, its name coming from Thomas Haney, who started a brick factory in 1878. The CPR was constructed in 1881 and brought hundreds of new settlers to the community. They started farming and logging in the surrounding area. The opening of the Lougheed Highway in 1931 was crucial to local improvement. The centre of Haney Place is in the larger picture. The smaller photo shows the Beast and Clock.

Ruskin

Ruskin was first settled in 1896. This small community located by the Stave River and Lougheed Highway is a part of the District of Maple Ridge. Ruskin is a wonderful recreational site, with a great fall fishing season and has a good view of a salmon spawning channel. There is a picnic site located immediately east of Ruskin Dam.

Stave Falls Dam

Stave Falls Dam was constructed in 1912. The historic Power House is open to the public, where visitors can experience an authentic 1912 generating station. The development of the dam continued from 1926 to 1929, and additional generators were installed in 1950. In 2000, upgrading of Stave Falls Dam was completed.

71

Langley Countryside

The agricultural centre of Langley is known as the "Countryside of Vancouver." Langley, with its major centres of Fort Langley, Aldergrove and Langley City, is located between Matsqui and Surrey. The Fraser Highway is a major route connecting Langley, Surrey, Vancouver, Matsqui and Abbotsford. This countryside picture was taken by Derby Reach Regional Park. Locals frequently shop at local farms and roadside vegetable farms to buy fresh produce, or pick berries and fruits themselves directly from the fields. The first settlers were William and Adam Innes, who came from Ontario. The original settlement was named "Innes Corners" and in 1911 was renamed to "Langley Prairie." The Township of Langley was incorporated in 1873.

Murrayville

Murrayville is a near neighbour to the city of Langley. It contains the Langley Municipal Airport, the Canadian Museum of Flight and Transportation, and Langley Memorial Hospital. Two smaller pictures show the Christian Life Assembly Church and Langley Secondary School, both located by 56 Avenue and McLeod Park.

Langley

An aerial picture of the Fraser Highway, the City of Langley and Langley Bypass. There are several shopping malls, such as the Willowbrook Shopping Centre and Langley Mall serving the needs of the community of Langley, concentrated next to sprawling car dealerships, supermarkets, restaurants and other commercial sites. The business centre of Langley is located around the Langley Bypass with central City Hall. Dozens of large stores are located in the area, near the site of Langley's first store and post office, from 1920 and 1921. Pictured prominently is the Chapters book superstore. Tens of thousands of books, magazines, calendars, CDs and other products arranged on well-marked shelves attract shoppers wishing to browse the meticulously organized store layout. Indigo, the largest national book retailer, is a Canadian company and it operates under the names of Indigo Books Music & more, Chapters, Coles, Smithbooks and World's Biggest Book Store.

Cloverdale

Part of Surrey, Cloverdale is known as the "Antique Capital of BC." Many heritage buildings date from 1910. In this picture, we see the Cloverdale United church.

Coquitlam

The Port Mann Bridge, Colony Farm Regional Park, Tree Island and the southern part of Coquitlam are visible in this picture. The Port Mann Bridge, a main connector for Greater Vancouver and the Lower Mainland, is a three-span steel-tied arch with an orthotropic deck. The five-lane bridge was completed in 1904 as part of the Trans-Canada Highway. Coquitlam, located on the opposite side of the Fraser River, was primarily a logging area and sawmill industry. The region became easily accessible for Vancouver when the Lougheed Highway was completed in 1950. Although the region is heavily urbanized on its slopes, there remain many relaxing spots, such as Minnekhana Regional Park, Mundy Park and the Poco Trail.

The Peace Arch

Standing astride the international boundary between Blaine, WA and Douglas, B.C., the Peace Arch was constructed by volunteers in 1920.

Walnut Grove

Pictured here, the industrial area of Walnut Grove.

Port Coquitlam

This aerial photograph displays Port Coquitlam slopes, Pitt Meadows, the Lougheed Highway, Pitt River and the Fraser River. Two sprawling suburbs east of Vancouver, Coquitlam and Port Coquitlam are located by Coquitlam Mountain. Coquitlam was incorporated as a municipality in 1891, and Port Coquitlam in 1913.

London Farm

Overlooking the southern arm of the Fraser River, London Heritage Farm offers lovely flower gardens, a barn with old farm equipment and six rooms with historic furniture, photographs, clothing and accoutrements. The farm was built in 1880 and is located by Dyke Road in Richmond. In its lovely tea room is served the farm's own blend of tea, the "London Lady."

Aldergrove Zoo

Aldergrove is the home of Vancouver's Zoo, located 30 minutes east of Vancouver by the Trans-Canada Highway. Tina the Asian Elephant welcomes visitors by the entrance. A Siberian Tiger, a Grizzly Bear and many other wild species draw families in the Fraser Valley to spend a day at this beautiful and educational attraction.

Port Moody

Belcarra Regional Park, Indian Arm and Port Moody are photographed on this page. Established at the end of North Road, Port Moody was the western terminus for the Canadian Pacific Railway. In 1886, the first transcontinental passenger train carrying 150 travellers arrived in Port Moody. The sawmill industry was established in 1905 and oil refinery development started in 1915. The name comes from Richard Moody, the Colonel of the Royal Engineers.

Burrard Inlet

The last stop on the north bank of the Fraser Valley is Vancouver. Together with the Fraser Valley, this area is called the Lower Mainland. North and West Vancouver, Burnaby, Surrey, Langley, Richmond and Delta are captured in detail in our Greater Vancouver book. This winter picture is taken from Cypress Bowl and shows North Vancouver and the whole Greater Vancouver area.

Annacis Island

Mainly industrial, Annacis Island is located in the Anneville Channel of the Fraser River, under the Alex Fraser Bridge.

New Westminster

Known as the Royal City and once the capital of British Columbia, New Westminster has an important role in the Fraser Valley. In the Gold Rush era, its port was the busiest in North America. The British government named the area a British Colony and dispatched a corps of Royal Engineers to establish law and order. Queen Victoria dubbed the settlement New Westminster and it remained British Columbia's capital until 1868, when it was superseded by the present day capital, Victoria.

Fraser Bridges

The Fraser River has always been an important travel route serving the West Coast and Fraser Valley. The Patullo Bridge, railway and SkyTrain Bridges can be seen high above the Fraser River from New Westminster's embankment—a popular place for weekend visitors to New Westminster's Quay Public Market.

78

Surrey–Mud Bay

When James Kennedy came into what is now Surrey, the area was occupied mostly by trappers and homesteaders. The first settlements were in Mud Bay, Brownsville and Cloverdale. Surrey, incorporated in 1879, held the reputation as the fastest growing community in all of Canada. Surrey has enjoyed tremendous booms in its town centres of Guildford, Cloverdale, Whalley, Sunnyside and Newton. The first picture shows Mud Bay, Nicomekl River, Elgin Heritage Park and Nico Wynd Golf Course. The area lies near White Rock.

Surrey–Sullivan

A new Surrey development and small shopping village by Panorama Drive and Highway 10.

Delta

The sunniest part of the Fraser Valley is Delta. Agriculture is a staple industry, thanks to rich and fertile soil. Originally, Delta was submerged marshland during the time of the Coast Salish settlement. The first Europeans arrived in Delta in 1859 and started to clear land for farming. Delta was founded by the Ladner brothers and was incorporated in 1879. The first mayor was William Ladner. Big floods in 1891 and 1895 inspired the settlers to the drainage project.

Ladner

The sunny and friendly neighbour of Tsawwassen and North Delta, Ladner is near the western end of the Fraser Valley. Pictured here is a residential area by Ladner Harbour Park. The name comes from the name of two brothers, William and Thomas Ladner, rich from the gold mines of Lillooet, who founded the community.

Ladner Reach

Delta's Island Park and the George Massey Tunnel's line are clearly visible in this aerial picture. Ladner Reach, the name of this part of the Fraser River, is located with its islands, Kirkland, Barber and Duck Islands, down from the tunnel line. The river above the tunnel is named Gravesend Reach.

Ladner

The older small town of Ladner is home to 20,000 residents. The waterfront has luxury town house developments where houses have their own moorage. The second picture was taken from Ladner Harbour and shows Old Government Wharf and the Ladner Yacht Club. Canoe Pass Village and a floating home development are very attractive. The third picture was taken in Ladner Downtown and shows Ladner Museum.

Queensborough

In its lowest part by New Westminster and around Annacis Island, the Fraser is a busy industrial river. Huge docks, the logging industry, commercial fishing, factories, shippers and warehouses are concentrated in Queensborough, next to residential areas.

Crescent Beach

Semiahmoo Park, just south along White Rock's beach is a popular picnic spot. Even a short walk on the beach or along the pier will reveal spectacular views to the south. Occasionally, even a pod of migrating whales can be spotted. This picture was taken on White Rock's Crescent Beach.

Surrey – North Delta

Part of White Rock, Surrey and North Delta are visible in this picture, taken from an airplane just above Semiahmoo Bay. On the skyline is Greater Vancouver and the Coastal Mountains.

White Rock

Just minutes away from the border, the city of White Rock is a sunny southerly suburb of Vancouver. With its small town feel and greater share of sunshine, White Rock is a popular spot to live and visit. Despite its small size, White Rock is the most cosmopolitan of Vancouver's suburbs. Along with its mild coastal climate comes a distinctly Californian atmosphere with modern ocean-side houses clinging to cliffs, and a bustling promenade of beach-side cafés. White Rock gets its name from the giant white boulder perched on its beach. According to legend, the rock was thrown across the Strait of Georgia by the son of a sea god. A visit to White Rock is a good way to get close to the sea. It is established from history that the first inhabitants arrived about 5000 years ago. The first cottage was built by Henry Thrift in 1892, and the Great Northern Railway was completed in 1909. White Rock now has about 18,000 residents.

Britannia Shipyard

Garry Point is located where the Fraser River empties into the Pacific Ocean. The past has left indelible marks here, where old boats were once moored, back to when the first Japanese fishermen started fishing here.

Van Dyke Trail

An old arm of the Fraser River in South Richmond is a regular afternoon stop for locals. Historic homes and moored boats bring forth memories of Steveston's past. The Van Dyke Trail is a favoured subject of photographers.

Richmond – Lulu Island

Richmond is a group of islands formed by the north and south arms of the Fraser River. On average, Richmond is less than two metres above sea level and many areas lie below. An interconnecting system of dikes keeps the ocean out, and these also serve as popular walking, jogging and cycling paths. The local silty earth has historically provided rich land for horticulture and agriculture, but Richmond is developing quickly as a secondary urban centre to Vancouver. Richmond gets its name from Hugh McRoberts, who established Richmond Farm on Lulu Island in 1861.

Sea Island

Taking off and landing over the ocean from Vancouver International Airport can be a spectacular way to glimpse the city's natural beauty. The airport was established in 1931, just over the Arthur Laing Bridge south of Vancouver.

Steveston

Steveston is an old part of the Fraser Valley. The historic but still active port is home to hundreds of fishing vessels and fishing companies. Thousands of tourists enjoy browsing between the boats and cozy gift shops. Some come to buy fresh fish directly from the boats or just capture scenes beautifully illuminated in the evening light. Numerous restaurants offer tasty seafood dishes. Fish and chips can be bought ready to eat in several waterfront kiosks.

Historic Steveston

The Gulf of Georgia Cannery is a landmark for fishermen, and is the oldest fish cannery in Greater Vancouver, constructed in 1894. An historic site which commemorates the west coast fishing industry is located on Bayview Street, at the mouth of Cannery Channel. It has an interesting collection of artifacts, machinery and short videos.

86

Sturgeon Bank

After 1368 kilometres through British Columbia, the waters of the Fraser River and its many tributaries empty into the Pacific Ocean, in the Strait of Georgia.

Strait of Georgia

The Iona Beach Regional Park, located in the north arm of the Fraser River is a great location for short sightseeing day trips. A 4 km walk down the spit provides views of the International Airport, river traffic and the occasional Bald Eagle feeding on fish near the shore. At dusk, people gather to watch some of the most beautiful sunsets over the Strait of Georgia.

* More photographs from other Canadian areas can be found in our line of 'CANADA' tourist books and Wall Calendars of Greater Vancouver, British Columbia, Canada, Sea to Sky, Atlantic Canada, Ontario, Southern Ontario, Toronto, Okanagan, Alaska-Yukon, Canadian Rockies and Historic British Columbia. Please see the back covers of our published books.

Photographer and Publisher

The author of this book, photographer Josef A. Hanus, founder of JH. Fine Art Photo Ltd., is one of the most accredited and celebrated scenery and wilderness photographers in Canada and North America. He has created over 12 photographic and tourist books and more than 80 different Canadian calendars since 1989. Now, Josef is working on a long line of new photographic books with the theme he loves the most—the natural beauty of Canada. His success with award winning photographs, best-selling lines of calendars and photographic books comes from very hard work. After Josef's graduation from the Art and Photography University in Europe, for many years he photographed for magazines and newspapers, and continued observing nature through the lens of his camera. By studying objects, he trained his taste for scenic views and his eye to the height of artistic professionalism. But his artistic vision is not the only result of his success. During the years, he has carefully selected his professional partners and patiently tested cameras and film material for his high quality work. The result of all this activity is seen in his products. People enjoy his photographic books and calendars because Josef loves to create them. Since 1997, Josef has worked with his son, Josef M. Hanus.

The Heart: JH. Fine Art Photo's published products are visibly marked with Josef's logo, a red heart with Canada's flag inside.